Natural Disasters

Hurricanes

by

Jean Allen

Consultant:
Stephen J. Colucci
Associate Professor of Atmospheric Sciences
Cornell University

CAPSTONE BOOKS
an imprint of Capstone Press
Mankato, Minnesota

Capstone Books are published by Capstone Press
151 Good Counsel Drive, P.O. Box 669, Mankato, Minnesota 56002
http://www.capstone-press.com

Library of Congress Cataloging-in-Publication Data
Allen, Jean, 1964–
    Hurricanes/by Jean Allen.
    p. cm.—(Natural disasters)
    Includes bibliographical references and index.
    Summary: Explains why hurricanes occur and describes the technology used to
study them, the damage they inflict, and some of the more famous hurricanes in
history.
    ISBN 0-7368-0587-7
    1. Hurricanes—Juvenile literature. [1. Hurricanes.] I. Title. II. Natural disasters
(Capstone Press)

QC944.2 .A55 2001
551.55'2—dc21   00-021414

Editorial Credits
Connie R. Colwell, editor; Timothy Halldin, cover designer and illustrator;
    Kia Bielke, illustrator; Heidi Schoof and Kimberly Danger, photo researchers

Photo Credits
Frank Siteman/Pictor, 34
Global Pictures, 20
Graeme Teague, 10, 30, 32, 36
Index Stock Imagery, 4, 43
International Stock/Warren Faidley, cover, 24, 26
Matt Robinson/Pictor, 16
Reuters/Oswaldo Rivas/Archive Photos, 6; Juan Carlos/Archive Photos, 8;
    Joe Skipper/Archive Photos, 38
Visuals Unlimited/Jeffrey Howe, 28; Seth S. Patterson, 41
World Perspectives/FPG International LLC, 12; Tom Carroll, 15

1 2 3 4 5 6 06 05 04 03 02 01

Table of Contents

Chapter 1

Hurricanes

Laura Isabel lived with her husband and three children in the Central American country of Honduras. Their home was in a small village near a river. In October 1998, heavy rains fell for several days. The river near the Isabel home began to rise. Strong winds began to blow.

The river rose above the villagers' homes. The Isabel family and other villagers climbed to the roofs of their homes to avoid the water. But the river continued to rise. It rose above the rooftops. The villagers were swept away by the water.

Laura Isabel clung to a floating tree to avoid drowning. Debris was floating all around her.

Strong winds and heavy rains occur during hurricanes.

Hurricanes can cause a great deal of damage.

She gathered some of this trash to make a small raft. Isabel floated on the raft for six days. The currents carried her 50 miles (80 kilometers) out to the ocean.

Isabel sometimes slept on the raft. She dreamed about her husband and children. She knew that they were dead. But she sang and talked to them as if they were with her.

An airplane pilot spotted Isabel floating in the ocean. The pilot dropped flares to mark Isabel's position. A helicopter pilot used these bright warning lights to guide the helicopter toward Isabel. The pilot then dropped a rope down to pick up Isabel. The airplane took her to a hospital near her home village.

A hurricane had changed Isabel's life. It also had changed much of Central America.

Hurricanes

Hurricanes are nature's largest storms. They can be as large as 600 miles (966 kilometers) wide. They can last for several days or weeks. Strong winds, heavy rains, and large waves occur during these storms. Violent windstorms called tornadoes also may form over land.

Hurricanes belong to a group of storms called tropical cyclones. A cyclone is a storm system with winds that blow in a circle around its center. Tropical cyclones form over tropical waters. These are the ocean's warmest areas.

Heavy rains from hurricanes can soften the ground and cause great splits in the Earth.

Tropical cyclones have different names in different parts of the world. Hurricanes are tropical storms that occur in the Atlantic Ocean or eastern Pacific Ocean. Tropical cyclones that occur in the western Pacific

Ocean are called typhoons. Tropical cyclones in the Indian Ocean are called cyclones.

Since the 1940s, weather service officials have named hurricanes. Names help prevent confusion when more than one hurricane occurs at a time. Hurricane names are repeated every several years. Officials retire the names of hurricanes that cause a great deal of damage or death. Retired hurricane names include Andrew, Camille, Bob, Fran, and Hugo.

Over the centuries, hurricanes have killed many people and destroyed many homes and businesses. Scientists work to develop methods to predict these storms. These methods may help protect property and lives.

Chapter 2

Why Hurricanes Happen

Hurricanes are a natural part of Earth's weather cycle. Certain weather conditions must exist for hurricanes to occur.

Air Pressure

The atmosphere is a layer of air that surrounds Earth. The atmosphere has weight. This weight on a surface is called air pressure.

Air pressure constantly changes. The air's temperature can cause these changes. The sun warms the air near the Earth. Warm air is less dense than cool air. Warm air rises. Cool air is more dense and sinks.

Certain weather conditions must exist for hurricanes to occur. ◁

11

Drops of water rise into the atmosphere and form clouds.

Temperature also affects the amount of moisture air can hold. Warm air can hold more moisture than cool air. Tiny drops of water escape with warm air. This process is called evaporation.

The warm air cools as it rises. The tiny drops of water clump together and form larger drops. This process is called condensation. The large drops combine with dust in the air to form clouds. The drops fall as rain when the clouds cannot hold any more moisture. Thunderstorms then may form.

The Equator

Tropical storms begin at the equator. This imaginary line around Earth's middle divides Earth in half. The northern half is called the Northern Hemisphere. The southern half is called the Southern Hemisphere.

The sun shines the strongest at the equator. The sun's rays heat the land and water near the equator. During summer, the water's temperature is about 80 degrees Fahrenheit (27 degrees Celsius).

The heated land and water warm the surrounding air. Condensation in the clouds warms the air further. This air then rises. Cool air flows in to take the warm air's place. This air movement causes wind.

The Coriolis Effect

The Coriolis Effect also affects the formation of hurricanes. The Earth rotates on its axis each day. This spinning motion causes wind to blow in curves. Fast winds curve more than slow winds. This occurrence is called the Coriolis Effect.

At the equator, the Coriolis Effect is weak. It does not cause the wind to curve much. But the Coriolis Effect is strong in areas surrounding the equator. Wind curves a great deal in these areas. Some wind curves so much that it begins to spin in a circle. This spinning wind can form hurricanes.

Parts of a Hurricane

The center of a hurricane is called the eye. This area is usually 5 to 20 miles (8 to 32 kilometers) wide. A hurricane's eye can be as large as 50 miles (80 kilometers) wide. The eye of a hurricane has calm winds and clear skies.

The eye wall is next to the eye. The eye wall forms a ring 20 to 30 miles (32 to 48 kilometers) wide. The wall has the strongest winds and the heaviest rain. Beyond the eye

cause damage in these areas. Hurricane winds can reach speeds of 75 miles (121 kilometers) per hour or more.

A hurricane's storm surge is the most deadly part of the storm. This huge wave of water occurs when the ocean's water level rises during a hurricane. The storm surge can be more than 18 feet (5.5 meters) high. The storm surge often damages property and injures or kills people. The storm surge causes about 90 percent of hurricane deaths.

Hurricanes can cause tornadoes. Tornadoes are much smaller and more intense than hurricanes. Their winds often are stronger than those of hurricanes. A tornado may measure 45 to 1,500 feet (14 to 457 meters) in diameter. Winds can exceed 300 miles (480 kilometers) per hour. Hurricane winds usually blow about 100 to 150 miles (161 to 241 kilometers) per hour. Most tornadoes last only a few minutes. But hurricanes can last for several days or weeks.

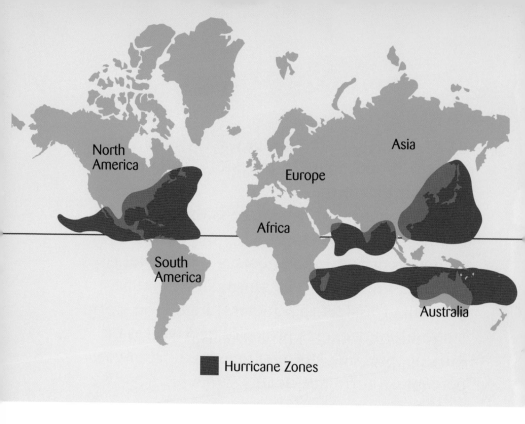

North America

Asia

Europe

Africa

South America

Australia

■ Hurricane Zones

Hurricanes also can cause floods. More than 12 inches (31 centimeters) of rain may fall during a hurricane. Rain may continue to fall even after hurricanes break apart. Floodwaters often damage property and injure or drown people and animals.

Hurricane Seasons
Hurricanes occur in seven large ocean areas called basins. The Atlantic basin includes the

Atlantic Ocean, the Gulf of Mexico, and the Caribbean Sea. This basin affects the United States and other countries in the Northern Hemisphere.

In the Atlantic basin, the hurricane season lasts from June to November. The largest number of hurricanes occur from mid-August to late October. The ocean waters near the equator are the warmest at this time.

In the Atlantic basin, about 100 tropical disturbances form each year. About 10 of these storms may reach the tropical storm stage. Six usually become hurricanes. But usually only two of these hurricanes strike land.

Throughout the world, the most tropical cyclones, typhoons, and hurricanes occur in September. May has the fewest.

Chapter 3

The Power of a Hurricane

Scientists have developed several methods to predict hurricanes and measure their damage. These methods include the Saffir-Simpson scale and the Dvorak technique.

The Saffir-Simpson Scale
In the United States, scientists rank hurricanes using the Saffir-Simpson scale. This scale measures a hurricane's ability to cause damage.

In the early 1970s, Herbert Saffir and Robert Simpson developed the Saffir-Simpson scale. Saffir was an expert on the effects of wind on buildings. Simpson was the director

Hurricanes' strong winds can damage property such as automobiles.

The Saffir-Simpson Scale

Hurricane Category	Wind Speeds	Storm Surge	Famous Hurricane in Category
1	74-95 mph 119-153 kph	4-5 feet 1.2-1.5 meters	Allison (1995) 0 deaths
2	96-110 mph 154-177 kph	6-8 feet 1.8-2.4 meters	Bonnie (1998) 3 deaths
3	111-130 mph 178-209 kph	9-12 feet 2.7-3.7 meters	Fran (1996) 34 deaths
4	131-155 mph 210-249 kph	13-18 feet 4-5.5 meters	Luis (1995) 17 deaths
5	Greater than 155 mph Greater than 249 kph	Greater than 18 feet Greater than 5.5 meters	Mitch (1998) More than 10,000 deaths

of the National Hurricane Center. He studied storm surges.

Categories on the Saffir-Simpson scale range from 1 to 5. Category 1 hurricanes are the weakest. Category 5 hurricanes are the strongest.

Category 1 hurricanes have winds from 74 to 95 miles (119 to 153 kilometers) per hour. The storm surge is 4 to 5 feet (1.2 to 1.5 meters) high. Category 1 storms cause some damage to shrubs, trees, and mobile homes.

Category 2 hurricanes have winds from 96 to 110 miles (154 to 177 kilometers) per hour. The storm surge is usually 6 to 8 feet (1.8 to 2.4 meters) high. Category 2 hurricanes cause damage to shrubs, trees, signs, and mobile homes. These hurricanes also may damage roofs, doors, and windows.

Category 3 hurricanes have winds from 111 to 130 miles (178 to 209 kilometers) per hour. The storm surge usually is 9 to 12 feet (2.7 to 3.7 meters) high. These hurricanes may damage homes and other buildings. Category 3

Scientists use satellite images to track hurricanes.

hurricanes also can blow down large trees. Rising water may cause damage to buildings and other structures.

Category 4 hurricanes have winds from 131 to 155 miles (210 to 249 kilometers) per hour. The storm surge usually is 13 to 18 feet (4 to 5.5 meters) high. Category 4 hurricanes can cause a great deal of damage to houses and other buildings. These hurricanes blow down shrubs, trees, and signs and destroy mobile homes. Some roads may be flooded. Flooding can make it difficult for people to evacuate, or leave, the area.

Category 5 hurricanes have winds that are more than 155 miles (249 kilometers) per hour. The storm surge is higher than 18 feet (5.5 meters). This category of hurricane causes severe damage. The winds overturn or destroy small buildings and mobile homes. Category 5 hurricanes severely damage or destroy roofs, windows, and doors. Trees, shrubs, and signs are blown down. Many roads may flood.

Hurricane Prediction

Scientists use satellites to help determine if hurricanes will occur. These spacecraft orbit Earth at an altitude of 22,000 miles (35,405 kilometers) above the equator. Satellites send images of weather patterns to scientists on Earth. The scientists then study the images for signs of hurricanes. Satellites also can show the size of a developed hurricane and its growth.

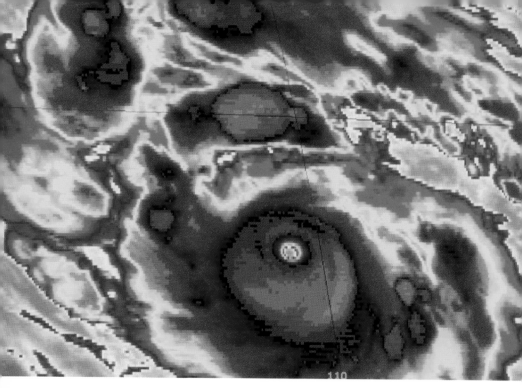

Scientists sometimes use infrared satellite images to indicate the intensity of a hurricane.

Scientists sometimes use the Dvorak technique to predict hurricanes. A scientist named Vern Dvorak developed this technique in the early 1970s. This technique matches current satellite images to previous storm patterns. The current satellite images sometimes appear similar to past storm pattern images. This similarity indicates that a hurricane may soon form.

Scientists also sometimes use infrared satellite images. These images indicate temperatures using colors. The temperature of the center of a hurricane and the surrounding cloud tops can indicate the intensity of a hurricane.

Hurricane Hunters

Satellite images can help scientists predict hurricanes. But scientists need more detailed information to make accurate predictions about a hurricane's path and intensity. They may depend on hurricane hunters to help find this information. These people fly airplanes near or into a hurricane. They then measure the weather conditions in order to learn about the storm.

In the Atlantic basin, the 53rd Weather Reconnaissance Squadron performs hurricane exploration. This U.S. Air Force Reserve unit is based at Keesler Air Force Base in Biloxi, Mississippi. The unit is the only organization in the world that regularly flies through hurricanes.

Raindrops

Hurricane hunters use aircraft to study hurricanes.

Hurricane hunters use WC-130H aircraft to perform their duties. These aircraft have computerized weather instruments. Hurricane hunters use this equipment to measure wind, air pressure, temperature, and humidity. They also determine the exact location of the storm's center. This information helps scientists accurately track the storm.

Scientists sometimes predict that a hurricane will hit land. The National Oceanic and Atmospheric Administration (NOAA) then studies the hurricane. NOAA pilots fly airplanes called SC-120s and WP-3D turboprops. These airplanes have more specialized instruments than the military planes.

In 1996, the NOAA added a Gulfstream IV business jet that had been converted to a research airplane. The jet can fly as high as 45,000 feet (13,700 meters). It also can travel more than 4,600 miles (7,400 kilometers) without refueling. This plane does not fly through the storm. It flies on top of it. The Gulfstream IV measures the winds from thousands of square miles or kilometers around the storm. These winds steer the storm. This information gives scientists a better idea of where the hurricane will travel.

Scientists monitor a hurricane by Doppler radar as the storm moves closer to land. This weather tool uses radio signals to provide

The National Weather Service monitors hurricanes to predict their paths.

visual images of weather patterns. Doppler radar provides accurate short-term warnings for the winds, tornadoes, and floods caused by hurricanes.

The information gathered from satellites, airplanes, and radar is entered into computers. This data helps scientists determine a hurricane's size, speed, and path. It also helps scientists determine wind speeds and the height of the storm surge.

Watches and Warnings

The National Weather Service (NWS) uses weather information to broadcast storm watches and warnings. Watches and warnings also provide information about tornadoes, floods, and high winds in specific areas.

Several categories of hurricane watches and warnings exist. Tropical storm watches mean that tropical storm conditions are possible within 36 hours. Tropical storm warnings indicate that tropical storm conditions are expected within 24 hours. Hurricane watches mean that hurricane conditions are possible within 36 hours. Hurricane warnings indicate that hurricane conditions are expected within 24 hours.

Chapter 4

Famous Hurricanes

Throughout history, hurricanes have caused a great deal of destruction. People study past hurricanes to learn ways to predict storms and prevent future damage.

Galveston, Texas

On September 8, 1900, a deadly hurricane struck the Texas coast from the Gulf of Mexico. This Category 4 hurricane's winds were estimated at 130 miles (209 kilometers) per hour.

The town of Galveston is located on Galveston Island near the Gulf of Mexico coast. At least 6,000 people died as a 20-foot (6.1-meter) storm surge hit the town. The wind

Throughout history, hurricanes have caused a great deal of destruction.

→ **Hurricane Andrew uprooted trees.**

and flooding destroyed two-thirds of all Galveston homes.

Hurricane Camille

Hurricane Camille was one of the most powerful hurricanes of the twentieth century. In August 1969, it developed in the Atlantic Ocean south of Cuba. The hurricane gained strength as it moved north to the Gulf of

Mexico near the Mississippi and Louisiana coasts. The storm's winds reached more than 200 miles (322 kilometers) per hour as it hit the coast. The storm killed 143 people in Mississippi and Louisiana.

Hurricane Camille weakened as it traveled north over land. But it still caused a great deal of damage. In Virginia, 153 people died from floods and landslides.

Hurricane Andrew

Hurricane Andrew is the third strongest hurricane in U.S. history. It developed in August 1992. Andrew's strength surprised even weather forecasters. The forecasters believed the storm would remain a tropical storm. But the wind speed increased from 50 to 140 miles (80 to 225 kilometers) per hour within just 48 hours. The storm was at full strength when it struck the Florida panhandle. This area is located on the Gulf of Mexico coast. The hurricane later hit south-central Louisiana.

Most of Hurricane Andrew's damage was caused by winds.

Most hurricane damage is caused by flooding or storm surges. But Andrew's damage was due to intense winds. The storm killed 58 people. Many of them were crushed by debris as their homes blew down. In Dade County, Florida, 160,000 people were left homeless. The storm also destroyed Homestead Air Force base near Homestead, Florida. Millions of people lost electric power. The power was not restored for two months in some areas.

The cost of Hurricane Andrew's damage was more than $25 billion. This figure made the storm the most expensive natural disaster in U.S. history.

Hurricane Mitch

In October 1998, Hurricane Mitch struck Central America. This Category 5 storm is considered the most destructive hurricane to hit the Western Hemisphere during the last 200 years. The storm moved through Honduras, Nicaragua, Guatemala, and El Salvador. Its winds reached 180 miles (290 kilometers) per hour. It remained at this level of strength for 33 hours. Some areas received as much as 6 feet (1.8 meters) of rain.

More than 10,000 people died during Hurricane Mitch. Millions were left homeless. Landslides buried entire villages. Banana, coffee, and tobacco crops were destroyed. Floodwaters reached the third floor in some downtown buildings. Many survivors clung to trees and rooftops for more than a week before being rescued.

Hurricane Mitch hit Naples, Florida, on November 1. It had weakened to a tropical storm by that time. It then caused five tornadoes. These tornadoes injured 65 people.

Chapter 5

Surviving a Hurricane

Today, warning systems help prevent many hurricane deaths. But the amount of property damage hurricanes cause has increased. More people are moving to coastal areas and building homes along the shoreline.

Population Increases

Many people choose to live along the coasts. In the United States, about 45 million people live along the Atlantic coastline from Maine to Texas. These numbers increase each year. Florida is among the nation's fastest growing states. This state also experiences the most hurricanes.

The amount of property damage hurricanes cause has increased in recent years.

Large numbers of people can make hurricane evacuations difficult. Roads often become jammed with vehicles trying to leave the area.

Preparing for a Hurricane

The best way to stay safe during a hurricane is to pay attention to watches and warnings. Even during a watch, people should behave as if a hurricane will happen. People will then be prepared if the watch suddenly becomes a warning.

People first should prepare their automobiles and homes for hurricanes. People should fill their automobiles with gasoline. These vehicles then will be ready for evacuation trips. People should have plywood on hand to cover windows and doors. Strong winds blowing through a building's windows and doors can tear off the roof. The walls of the building then may collapse. People also should bring lawn furniture, garbage cans, bicycles, garden tools, and other outdoor equipment inside. Strong winds can toss these objects in the air. The objects may hit people, vehicles, and buildings.

People should keep radios or televisions tuned to a local station for storm reports. They should

People should prepare for hurricanes by nailing plywood over their windows.

always follow the instructions of disaster officials or police. If possible, people should evacuate during the day. They should inform neighbors of their evacuation plans. They also should notify a family member or friend outside the warning area.

Some people should always evacuate during hurricane warnings. These people live in mobile homes, high-rise apartments, near rivers, or on coasts or islands. These places are not safe during hurricanes.

Safety During a Hurricane

Some people may choose to remain in their homes during less severe hurricanes. People sometimes want to look out windows or doors to watch the storm. People even may want to go outside. But these are not safe practices. Winds can shatter windows and rip doors from their frames. Glass and flying debris can hit people. People should stay inside and away from windows and doors. They should lie under a heavy table or bench for protection from falling objects.

People sometimes think the storm is over when the hurricane's eye passes. But this is not true. The storm is still dangerous. Winds blow from the opposite direction when the other side of the hurricane passes over. These winds may put more stress on buildings that are still standing after the first part of the storm. These buildings may collapse.

Safety after a Hurricane

Hurricanes still can cause injury and death after they have passed. Floodwaters may flow for several days. Downed power lines may cause injury or start fires. City water supplies may be contaminated. Gas leaks might occur. Roads and bridges may be washed out or blocked with boats, cars, trees, or debris. Emergency vehicles may not be able to get to emergency sites.

Relief organizations often offer assistance after hurricanes.

People should continue to take safety precautions after hurricanes. They should continue to listen to radio or television reports. City and state officials will offer updates on storm conditions and necessary actions. The military and relief organizations such as the Red Cross often assist in rescue efforts and in setting up shelters.

Hurricanes are nature's largest and most destructive storms. People cannot prevent these storms. But they can prepare for hurricanes and follow safety precautions to help prevent damage and injury.

→ **Words to Know**

air pressure (AIR PRESH-ur)—the weight of the air on a surface

cyclone (SY-clone)—a storm with strong winds that blow around a center

debris (duh-BREE)—the remains of something that has been destroyed

devastate (DEV-uh-state)—to badly damage or destroy

evacuation (ee-vak-yoo-AY-shun)—the removal of large numbers of people leaving an area during a time of danger

evaporate (i-VAP-uh-rate)—to turn liquid into vapor or gas

satellite (SAT-uh-lite)—a device made by people that circles around the Earth; satellites are used to gather and send information.

tornado (tor-NAY-doh)—a violently rotating column of air that extends from a thunderstorm to the ground

To Learn More

Erlbach, Arlene. *Hurricanes.* Chicago:
Children's Press, 1993.

Hood, Susan. *Hurricanes!* New York: Simon
Spotlight, 1998.

Kahl, Jonathan D. *Storm Warning: Tornadoes
and Hurricanes.* How's the Weather?
Minneapolis: Lerner Publications, 1993.

→ Useful Addresses

Central Pacific Hurricane Center
Nation Weather Service Forecast Office
University of Hawaii at Manoa
Department of Meteorology
2525 Correa Road
Honolulu, HI 96822

Joint Typhoon Warning Center
425 Luapele Road
Pearl Harbor, HI 96860

National Hurricane Center
11691 SW 17th Street
Miami, FL 33165-2149

National Weather Service, NOAA
1325 East-West Highway
Silver Spring, MD 20910

Internet Sites

The 53rd WRS
http://hurricanehunters.com

Hurricanes—FEMA for Kids
http://www.fema.gov/kids/hurr.htm

National Hurricane Center Tropical Prediction Center
http://www.nhc.noaa.gov

NCEP—The Saffir-Simpson Hurricane Scale
http://www.nhc.noaa.gov/aboutsshs.html

Index